IMS:
A Framework for Integrated Management Systems

Integrated Management Systems Series

The Integrated Management Systems (IMS) series of books provides practical guidance and advice on integrating the systems operating within an organization. The IMS series provides a framework into which additional management systems can be incorporated.

Each volume is written by an acknowledged expert in the field. The series editor is David Smith of iMS Risk Solutions Ltd, who has been involved in writing management system standards since the early 1990s and is himself the author of a number of BSI books on the subject.

IMS: A Framework for Integrated Management Systems
IMS: Implementing and Operating Using PAS 99
IMS: The Excellence Model
IMS: Creating a Manual
IMS: Customer Satisfaction
IMS: Continual Improvement through Auditing
IMS: Risk Management for Good Governance
IMS: Information Security
IMS: Managing Food Safety

Integrated Management Systems Series

IMS: A Framework for Integrated Management Systems

Background to PAS 99 and its application

David Smith and Rob Politowski

iMS Risk Solutions Ltd

BSi
Business Information

First published in the UK in 2007

by
BSI
389 Chiswick High Road
London W4 4AL

First published in 2001 as *IMS: The Framework*

Typeset in Gill Sans and Century Schoolbook by Monolith
Printed in Great Britain by Berforts Group. www.berforts.com

British Library Cataloguing in Publication Data
A catalogue record for this book is available from the British Library

ISBN 978-0-580-50950-6

Acknowledgements

The authors wish to acknowledge the sterling support provided by Chris Millidge in the production of this book. His insightful comments and editing have been a consistent source of help and inspiration. Christine Cox and her colleagues at BSI have provided the continual encouragement necessary to complete the project.

Contents

1. Introduction

In an ideal world an organization would have one simple management system covering all aspects of its operation. In practice many organizations that have formal management systems have kept their systems independent, thereby adding to costs, increasing bureaucracy and reducing effectiveness. This situation has arisen because of the perceived difficulties in integrating management system requirements from the various management system specifications.

Since the publication of the first edition of this book (previously titled *IMS: The Framework*) there has been a significant increase in the number of management system standards and specifications that organizations may need to adopt. There are now standards on information security, food safety etc. that are becoming important. There are also guides produced or being produced such as BS 8900:2006, *Guidance for managing sustainable development* and ISO/CD 31000, *General guidelines for principles and implementation of risk management* to which organizations may wish to subscribe. PAS 99:2006 – *Specification of common management system requirements as a framework for integration* has been produced in response to a market need for a solution to the problem of managing multiple systems. The background to this specification and how it may be applied is covered within this book.

The concept of a truly integrated management system (IMS) is one that has generated increasing interest and appeal over recent years. For many organizations their first experience of a documented system in accordance with a management system standard was the implementation of a quality system, generally ISO 9001 or its predecessors. When they subsequently came to implement an environmental management system, or perhaps health and safety, the similarities in the structure suggested that some form of integration between the two ought to be possible. It appeared that there also should be advantages in avoiding parallel requirements both internally in matters of control, audit etc. and externally in respect of multiple assessments and surveillances. In practice it was found that there were difficulties – the pieces of the jigsaw would fit together in some places but not in others.

This book reviews the background to the current situation and the book of PAS 99. It shows the reason for this approach, which enables integration to become a reality, not merely between two standards such as ISO 9001 and ISO 14001 but as part of an overall system for the company. It can be used to ensure that the common requirements found in specifications such as ISO 9001, ISO 14001, BS OHSAS 18001, BS ISO/IEC 27001, BS EN ISO 22000 and BS ISO/IEC 20000 can be addressed in a consistent way. Some organizations may see the framework as being one that can embrace all their requirements, although PAS 99 makes no claim to be a business management system or an IMS.

This book helps to identify the benefits of such an approach and emphasizes the key features for making a system effective. In the UK, the Government's occupational health and safety (OH&S) agency recommends that OH&S management should be part of the overall business system. Internationally, the Organisation for Economic Co-operation and Development (OECD) has given guidance on how to integrate ISO 9001, ISO 14001 and BS OHSAS 18001 in its publication *Integrated Management Systems (IMS) – Potential Safety Benefits Achievable from Integrated Management of Safety, Health, Environment and Quality (SHE&Q)*, thereby encouraging organizations to think this way. This book does not claim to be a 'how to' manual. The details of the specific requirements of particular management system standards have been covered in other publications in this series. What it does seek to do is to describe a framework that enables the incorporation of any chosen standards or codes relating to any specific discipline.

2. Terms and definitions

Many readers of this book are likely to be well versed in the vocabulary and style of international standards, but it is helpful to clarify meanings in order to avoid confusion. International standards tend to define words to convey a specific sense and sometimes there are variations in meaning between different standards.

Definitions can sometimes be misleading. The term 'management system', for example, can be defined in a few words, but such a definition does not convey the full meaning of the term to someone who has not met it before; an explanation is needed rather than a definition; see Chapter 5 if you are new to the idea of a 'management system'.

For convenience, the relevant definitions used in PAS 99 are included below:

3.1 aspect
characteristic of an activity, product or service that has or can have an impact (see 3.4)

...

3.3 document
information and its supporting medium

3.4 impact
effect on the organization's policy commitments and objectives, its interested parties, the organization itself and/or on the environment

3.5 interested party
person or group concerned with or affected by the activities, products and/or services of an organization

3.6 management system
system(s) to establish policy and objectives and to achieve those objectives

3.7 procedure
specified way to carry out an activity or a process

3.8 process
set of interrelated or interacting activities which transforms inputs into outputs

3.9 risk
likelihood of an event occurring that will have an impact on objectives

For additional explanation and discussion on all of the above terms please refer to PAS 99, Annex A.

3. The different approaches

The main models that are used in management system standards and specifications are based upon the process approach in some cases and on plan-do-check-act (PDCA) in others. There are compelling reasons for these, and they are sometimes seen as conflicting, but it will be shown that the two can be compatible.

The process approach

ISO 9001 utilizes a process approach for quality management. The intention is to ensure that processes are in place for all operations. The instructions for following the process are often in the form of a procedure. If those procedures are followed, then the system should yield the desired result.

The current edition of the quality standards ISO 9001:2000 and ISO 9004:2000 take a broader view of quality within organizations than in earlier versions. It is no longer restricted just to the physical quality of the outputs. Moves in this direction had already been made in many organizations in the application of Total Quality Management (TQM) and other quality management systems.

The PDCA approach

Management system standards and specifications such as ISO 14001 and BS OHSAS 18001 use the PDCA approach. This has given rise to some confusion and the belief that the two approaches are incompatible and mutually exclusive. As will be seen this is not the case, and the

Karapetrovic et al. (2006) study showed that organizations have found it useful to accommodate both approaches.

The PDCA sequence is intrinsic in any control system. First there is the decision on what the final objective of the operation is, and how it is intended to achieve it. This is the 'plan' stage, which is inherently risk-based.

The second stage is to carry out the processes by which the objective is to be achieved. This is the 'do' stage and is followed by a 'check' stage to confirm that the objective has been achieved.

The 'act' stage covers two operations. If the 'check' stage has shown a failure to achieve the objective completely, the 'plan' and 'do' stages need to be re-examined to assess where the failure has occurred, and the necessary changes made. If the 'check' stage confirmed that the objective has been attained, the review should consider how the whole process can be improved to achieve the objective better or more efficiently. Continual improvement must be the aim of every organization. 'Act' therefore involves a review of the achievement and taking steps to improve it.

Because the PDCA cycle is inherent in just about every activity that any organization does, from the simplest operation to the overall results of the organization, it applies just as much to a system built originally on a process approach as to any other.

Recognition of the universality of the PDCA cycle will do much to remove many of the apparent difficulties that may arise in the integration of management systems. It recognizes the essentials of a simple system and enables complex systems to be broken down into their simpler sub-systems where analysis is easier.

Harmonization of the two approaches

The process system, now principally used in ISO 9001, is a helpful way of identifying the critical issues that need to be controlled. It can be encompassed within the PDCA framework and helps to integrate the two approaches. It is useful for any organization to have process maps of its operation as these can be used to identify those activities that can critically impact on the quality of the product, the environment, personnel etc.

For those approaching the subject from a quality background, the risk-based PDCA approach seems at odds with the framework proposed in ISO 9001. However, some organizations, particularly those in the engineering sector, will have found Failure Mode and Effects Analysis

(FMEA) a useful tool. In the chemical sector, hazard analysis and operability studies (HAZOPS) are used, and in the food sector hazard analysis and critical control points (HACCP). These are risk-based approaches for managing quality within an ISO 9001 framework.

So, a risk-based approach similar to that used in the PDCA cycle is common in many organizations in industry. They may not be aware of the fact that their approach is risk-based, but even quality relies on determining what will satisfy the customer's needs at a cost the provider can afford and still make a return.

It can be seen from the hundreds of companies operating to the ISO 9001 system that combining the process approach with the PDCA risk-based approach gives added benefits and no disadvantages (see Karapetrovic et al.).

4. Why consider an integrated management system?

A management system exists to bring benefit to the organization in which it operates. Where formal management systems have been implemented separately (e.g. quality, environment) there will be duplications, additional costs and even conflicts.

PAS 99 states in the introduction:

> This PAS has been produced to help organizations to achieve benefits from consolidating the common requirements in all management system standards/specifications and managing these requirements effectively. The benefits may include:
>
> a) improved business focus;
> b) a more holistic approach to managing business risks;
> c) less conflict between systems;
> d) reduced duplication and bureaucracy;
> e) more effective and efficient audits both internally and externally.

From a business perspective, there should be only one management system. The aim should therefore be to develop a cohesive system that supports the day-to-day operations and delivers what the organization needs. The system should not be a tome of procedures that drives the organization. The aim of implementing an IMS must be that of delivering the organization's needs in the simplest and most effective manner.

For instance, it does not make sense to provide instructions or training on how to do a job and then to provide separate instructions on how the task should be done safely or how to dispose of the waste. The employee doing the job just wants clear, practical training and instructions on how to do the task so that it satisfies all those parties that have an interest in the outcome. There is also the added benefit that introduction of change in one area, such as 'a new paint system being applied to widgets' does not go ahead without reference to quality, environment, and health and safety issues. The system is proactive, preventing difficulties and mistakes rather than correcting them after the event.

In short, the case for integration is one of simple economics and organizational efficiency and effectiveness. However, this cannot be achieved by taking the different management systems already in place (e.g. quality, health and safety) and wrapping them together into one set of manuals. Integration must be carefully planned and implemented in a balanced way.

5. The basis of an integrated management system

The term 'management system' describes a very simple concept: it is the means by which any enterprise sets out to achieve its objectives. Every enterprise, even a sole trader, has a management system. The term refers to managing the business not the people in it; someone may be called a 'manager' even if he or she has no subordinates to manage.

In essence, any enterprise takes inputs and adds value to produce a desired output that is appreciated by a customer. The term 'customer' here refers to the user of the output, not necessarily the person who has paid for it. Government departments, charities and many other organizations provide a service that is paid for by one set of people and used by another set. In the wider context, a worker can be seen as a customer for OH&S arrangements that work for his or her benefit.

The simplest form of enterprise is one where one person is selling his or her services, perhaps as a casual handyman or a management consultant. Although there is no question of conversion of materials in such an enterprise, there are still a number of activities to be managed – find customers, agree rates, obtain tools, collect money, pay taxes and so on. He or she will have a system for doing each of these things. That system will probably not be written down or formalized in any way and possibly not even thought about much in advance, but the fact that the service is performed and paid for by a satisfied customer means that there is a system and that it works.

The larger and more complex the enterprise the more elaborate the management system. The probability is that it will still not be written down or even regarded as an enterprise-wide system that leads to the development of subsystems dealing with particular areas of activity. The company accountant will almost certainly have an elaborate and well-documented system for recording all the money aspects of the firm's activities. There will be another system covering the purchasing of materials – the selection of suppliers, placing orders, checking goods in, monitoring performance, supplier payment and so on. Such a system may be formalized and written down, or may be developed ad hoc as further rules and records are found to be necessary. The personnel department may have another system, for recruiting employees, training, salary payment and so on.

All these are part of the overall management system of the enterprise, but it is only rarely that they are brought together in the way that they are seen as a single overall system. The company may well have an overall organization chart and a system of job descriptions defining everyone's responsibility and accountability but, below that, fragmentation and specialization usually take place.

In the traditional company/organization there will be at the top a board of management that meets regularly and contains representatives responsible for every aspect of the company's operations. It is often only at that level that the activities of the organization can be seen as a whole.

Benefits of management systems

This separation of systems by function has obscured their fundamental unity of purpose, which is to enable the enterprise to meet its objectives. This was the principal reason that enterprises ran into difficulties when they first started implementing quality management systems (ISO 9001 and its predecessors).

A few manufacturers eagerly adopted quality standards because they saw how they would benefit their business. Some enterprises, especially the smaller ones, adopted them reluctantly because their customers insisted on it. Many regarded this as an imposition. They had been running a successful business for a long time without any complaints from apparently totally satisfied customers and did not see why this could not continue. For the first time they had to have a formal system with written procedures, records and so on. They also had to install a system that did not line up with their functional organization. Although almost exclusively about the quality of the output, the standard extended beyond the conversion process to other functions, such as purchasing.

However, once this system was in and working, the benefits to the operation of the company – quite apart from keeping customers happy –

became obvious. Many said that for the first time they had got their stock room and production under control and they had been able to identify weaknesses in their organization. One managing director admitted that for the first time he felt that he actually knew what was going on in his company. Suppliers often gave better service and even customers treated them with more respect.

Adding more systems

Some realized that the benefits of the system could be extended and become the basis of a company-wide management system. What was good for the quality of the product was also good for the other operations within the company, such as marketing, book keeping, sales and personnel. Some recognized that within the organization there are many internal supplier–customer relationships to which the quality system principles could equally apply. The system could therefore become the basis of a unified system for the enterprise.

For many, however, the quality management system remained the only formalized system. Other systems existed within the individual functions, such as in sales and accounts, but they were not seen as being part of any unified whole. In this situation, when additional management systems needed to be introduced – environmental, for example – this was done either as a further stand-alone system in parallel with quality or, because of the obvious similarities between the two, attempts were made to integrate environmental management with the quality system. For the most part it was still not recognized that the real need was to integrate them both into an overall management system that would include all the activities within the enterprise.

The problems become greater when additional management systems are added – perhaps OH&S, then human resources management, and then maybe risk management. It is perfectly feasible to integrate these with all the existing systems. However, the real benefit comes from recognizing that they form part of the overall management system, covering all the enterprise's activities, and that these additional requirements are no more than specialist developments relating to some specific aspect of the operations. A lot of the problems envisaged when trying to merge the stand-alone systems then become quite insignificant.

Organization

PAS 99 does not propose that the model it gives is the only possible management system or that it should be the business management system. The IMS that an organization adopts will relate to its needs. The integration or alignment will be determined by what suits the organization best, bearing in mind the complexity of the organization and the business needs. The PAS 99 framework offered here, however, can be used as a framework for managing all business risk – should the organization choose to do so.

The basis of a management system

Take the simple example of a husband and wife partnership selling hot dogs from a mobile van that sites itself close to a soccer stadium when there are home games. They are competing with other vans selling similar products, at similar prices. All use gas cylinders to provide the energy for cooking.

These small businesses need to supply a product of consistent quality to retain customers and attract new ones. They need to control their raw materials, the cooking process and the presentation. They need to ensure that the health and safety arrangements are sound and that they do not cause environmental nuisance. Strict food hygiene regulations require that they demonstrate a sound hazard analysis and critical control points (HACCP) system.

So, in this simple example some arrangements are needed that relate to ISO 9001, ISO 14001, BS OHSAS 18001 and BS EN ISO 22000:2005. The arrangements may well not be full management systems that would satisfy any of these standards, but the principles of each will have been addressed.

It would obviously not be sensible for this business to have four formal management systems. The partners need integrated arrangements for controlling the main risks associated with food hygiene, quality of the product, health and safety of themselves and any assistants as well as the general public, and the environment.

Traditionally, quality management systems have been concerned almost exclusively with the quality of the product. If an activity of the organization did not affect the quality of the output then no account had to be taken of it in implementing ISO 9001. Should the company then decide, for instance, to adopt the requirements of an OH&S management system and to integrate it with its quality management system, immediate problems arise. No part of the company's activities can be excluded from the requirements of the health and safety system. This means that a whole new set of activities will need to be covered by the system, which was primarily designed to take care of the quality of the output. However, if the enterprise has been far-sighted enough to recognize in the quality management system a blueprint that could profitably be applied to every activity of the company, many of these difficulties need not arise. If process maps exist and the organization has processes in place for monitoring, documentation, audits, training, management review etc. then the extension of the systems to manage a new discipline is not such a great task.

The ISO management system standards do not conflict with each other; neither do they ever ask that an organization does something that does not make sense or that is inappropriate to its operation. Increasingly, care is being taken by ISO to ensure that management system standards adopt a common terminology and, in so far as it is consistent with their purpose, a common format, making it easier to recognize the best path to integration.

Organizational changes have been taking place in recent years. In all types of enterprise the strict vertical separation by function is disappearing. Whole levels of management have disappeared and those that remain are largely multifunctional. One consequence is that managers now more readily appreciate the value of company-wide systems crossing boundaries that were previously delineated strictly by function. They have to be multifunctional and cannot segregate their job into compartments, as was once the practice. The pressure for growth of purely functional systems has gone and instead managers are now able to take a much wider view of the company's activities. It can therefore be confidently predicted that there will be a greater acceptance of the benefits of company-wide management systems for operational purposes, which will facilitate the incorporation of new specialist management systems (risk management, security, human resources management etc.) as they come along.

If an organization identifies and addresses the issues within its overall management system, it will find that it has a system very similar in structure to that demanded within management system standards. PAS 99 formalizes those common requirements found in management system standards/specifications.

6. The background to integrated management system standards

The first formal management system standard was the quality standard ISO 9001 and its predecessors – in the UK, BS 5750, and before that the Defence Standards of the Ministry of Defence. Tens of thousands of organizations adopted the quality standard and became certificated, principally in the manufacturing area to start with, but later extending to services, education, local government and even the professions. Certification to the standard became an almost universal badge of respectability, and was increasingly demanded by customers.

The next standard to appear concerned the environment. A number of guides and codes were produced, culminating in the ISO 14000 series. Some of the organizations that sought to implement this environmental standard were already working to ISO 9001 and had OH&S systems in place; companies began to ask whether the two or more systems could be managed as a single entity. They were influenced not only by the internal organizational benefits of such arrangements, but also by the desirability of avoiding multiple assessments and surveillance visits. Some organizations wanted the two standards to be replaced by a single standard embracing the requirements of both or of any new standard that was developed. Others considered that they should be kept entirely separate. Still more thought that future editions should move towards alignment to enable common management by those organizations that wished it. Prior to the publication of the 2000 edition of the quality standard, an organization could define the scope of ISO 9001 within its activities, whereas the ISO 14000 environmental standards could not be so limited: it applied across the organization.

It was recognized that as time went by, there could well be a succession of management systems standards, dealing with other aspects of an organization's activities with unlimited scope for complication if there were to be no agreement on the relationship between different standards. To take the discussion forward BSI carried out a survey in 1996 to assess the 'UK need for compatible international standards for quality, environmental and other management systems'. The questions related to the environmental and quality standards, asking for the views of users on whether ISO should aim to achieve greater compatibility between the two; whether it should aim to achieve integration or alignment; or whether they should be kept entirely separate. It went on to ask how future ISO management system standards should be developed, and whether 'one-stop' certification was a desirable objective.

The questionnaire was circulated to major users of the standards, trade associations, professional institutions, government departments and consultants. The results were not conclusive in all respects, but they did strongly support the need for greater compatibility between the standards with the ultimate possibility of one-stop certification and surveillance.

Further consultation led to a report (MacGregor Associates, 1997) recommending that whilst total integration (in the sense of having an overall standard covering quality, environment etc.) was not a practical proposition, future editions of management system standards should work towards alignment. Definitions and vocabulary should be consistent and a common structure followed so that the common elements could, if required, be managed as an entity with the specific requirements being clear for each discipline. These recommendations have since become generally accepted and the latest edition of the ISO 9000 series has taken a significant step forward in achieving compatibility with other management system standards.

It is expected that management system standards will in future be written (or revised) so that they have a common element structure, using the same terms and definitions wherever possible. This will allow organizations to integrate, interface or align to the extent that suits them. Diagrammatically, this can be seen in Figure 6.1.

It is impractical to consider a single comprehensive management system standard. Constant changes and new standards arising would make it continually out of date, and not all the contents would necessarily be relevant to a particular organization.

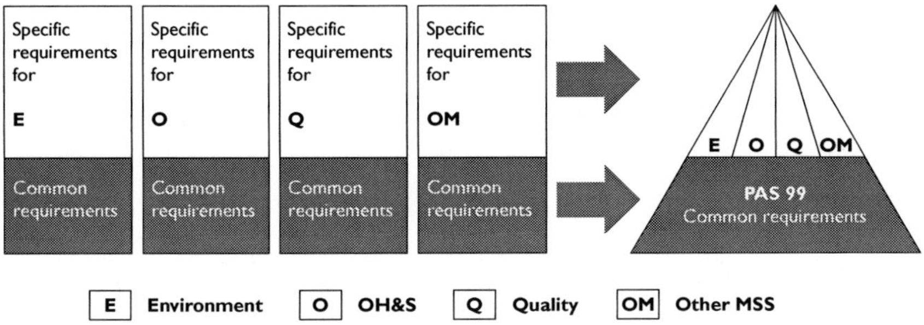

Source: PAS 99, p.iv

Figure 6.1 – Illustration of how common requirements of multiple management system standards/specifications can be integrated into one common system

7. The common requirements of management systems

The main elements of the framework for integrating management systems or for developing an IMS within an organization can be grouped as follows:

Policy Planning	}	Plan
Implementation and operation	}	Do
Performance assessment	}	Check
Improvement Management review	}	Act

This is shown in the cycle in Figure 7.1, overleaf, indicating the continual improvement implicit in this approach.

Those who are familiar with management systems terminology and the implementation of systems will be aware of the contents of the many sub-elements contained within the individual elements, although the order is different to that found in ISO 9001, ISO 14001, BS OHSAS 18001 and ISO 27000 for instance. The elements and sub-elements have been ordered to facilitate integration of management systems should the user so wish. The order of the sub-elements is given in Chapter 9 with some explanation of what is sought to meet the needs of the element. The formal wording of the common integrated management elements and sub-elements is given in Appendix 1. There are specific sub-elements in the various management system standards that are not covered here. To implement an integrated system, these specific requirements need to be addressed for each of those specifications that the organization subscribes to.

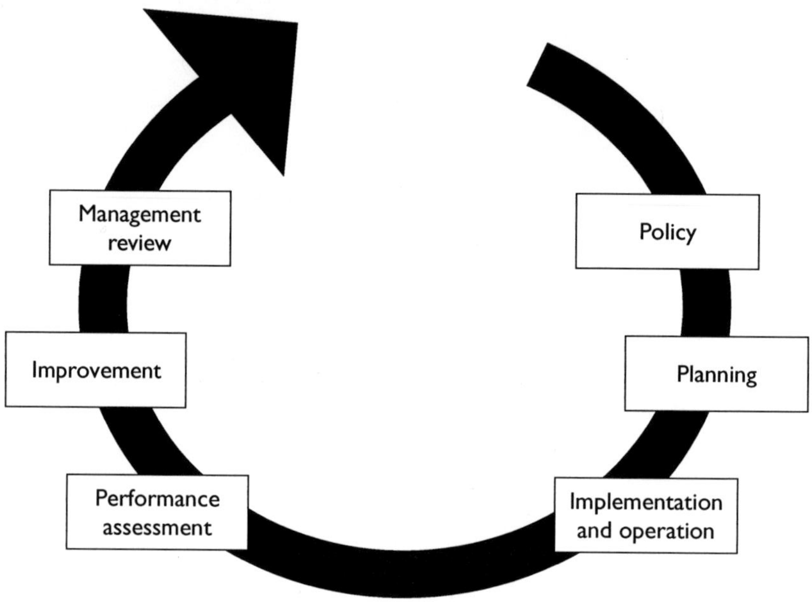

Figure 7.1 – The common requirements of management systems

8. Making an integrated management system work

Even a well-produced and documented management system is a complete failure if it is not used. There are a number of lessons to be learnt that can help those starting on this route to ensure their system is used and is not just dusted off when inspections or audits are taking place.

Obviously leadership, motivation and commitment to the system are vital. If these three elements are in place then employees will make the system work. If the system is poorly conceived and developed, frustration will undermine the commitment and motivation. So there needs to be a balance to ensure that the system helps the organization to achieve its objectives and yet does not impose a bureaucratic burden.

Characteristics of an organization with an effective integrated management system

An organization that has implemented an effective IMS will have the following key features:

- Everyone knows that top management is leading the project for integration.
- Everyone knows what the objectives of the organization are and how it is seeking to achieve them.
- Everyone knows what their job is, what results are expected of them and how those results are measured and assessed.
- Everyone knows that they will receive adequate training for the tasks they are asked to perform.

- Everyone knows that continual improvement in all aspects of work-based activity is an objective of the organization and hence efforts and suggestions to achieve improvement in any area are welcomed.
- Everyone knows that top and line management supports and participates in integrated management and that workforce training and development has an essential part to play.
- Everyone feels involved in the work of the organization – through their ownership of specific tasks.

The way to achieve this organizational 'culture' is a separate subject, but one of the main requirements, top management support and participation, is outlined below.

Top management support and participation

For an IMS implementation project to succeed, top management within an organization needs to generate a clear picture of what is expected of it. An IMS, operating efficiently and effectively, should bring significant financial and operational benefits. Top management needs to believe this and to commit to achieving these benefits.

The purpose of implementing any management system is to bring improvement to the organization, but all too often the expected benefits are not made clear to everyone who is going to be involved. The new system may then be seen by some as just an additional chore.

It is important for a positive culture to be established throughout the organization. This common culture, stemming from the shared values of the senior decision makers, is an essential element of an IMS, as their shared values are implicit in every act or decision. To achieve this commitment, top management needs to identify and explain the business benefits and to encourage ownership throughout the organization. Remember that for every pair of hands you get a brain free and even the most junior employee can make an important contribution to the organization if they are offered the opportunity.

The integrated system in practice

An overall management system requires planning and needs the objectives and the methods of operational control specified. It requires documentation control, records, audit in some form, and a periodic review.

Each of the specific management system standards will require these basic provisions, probably with the addition of some specific provisions relating to that particular discipline such as quality or health and safety. None of these extra provisions will conflict with each other or with those already existing in the overall company management system.

It is clear that the principal difficulties that organizations have encountered have arisen because they have attempted to integrate systems of specific disciplines with each other, rather than seeing them as part of the overall company management system.

To overcome this difficulty requires recognition that there is indeed a management system for the organization as a whole. It may not be formally structured as such, but it will certainly exist. Equally certainly it will contain in one form or another the essential elements specified above – planning, policy, review etc. It is this overall system that should be formalized first before attempting to integrate further management systems relating to a specific discipline. This may seem an intimidating prospect to an organization that has never viewed its management system in this way, but effort at this stage will greatly reduce difficulties later when extending the system to encompass further disciplines.

Quality standards arose from a demand from industry to enable them to meet better the requirements of their customers. The other more recent management system standards have similarly come into being because of a demand for them, principally from industry but also from other potential users. None is compulsory, and this is unlikely to change, although some have been developed to assist users in meeting legal requirements that *are* compulsory, e.g. OH&S. Users have adopted these standards because they have found it profitable to do so. It is likely that the list of such standards will grow for exactly the same reasons. Risk management, customer complaints, human resources and information security are just some areas where organizations will find it profitable to adopt management system standards – probably not all of them in any one company, just those that are relevant to the profitability of the organization. Those that are adopted will need to be incorporated into the overall company system.

It is no good believing that if you start by integrating quality and environmental, for example, these two can by their addition grow automatically into a company-wide management system. They will not, because between them they affect only a fraction of the company's total activities. The organization should recognize that there is an overall management system and it is into this that new disciplines need to be incorporated.

PAS 99 recognizes that all organizations have a management system and that they need to incorporate the formal requirements from management system standards within it for effective and efficient management. The specification identifies core requirements, as outlined in Chapter 9, which can be formalized within the existing management system. Having achieved this, it is much easier to embrace any new specifications without causing conflict.

9. PAS 99: The framework and requirements

General requirements (Clause 4.1)

This introductory element establishes what the management system needs in general terms. It states that an organization should ascertain the processes needed for management and where these occur throughout the organization.

The introduction in effect asks that the organization implements all the elements of the PDCA management system to ensure that it is working efficiently and to continually improve the performance.

Management system policy (Clause 4.2)

This is the statement of commitment and vision by the organization; it should not be a meaningless piece of prose sited conveniently for customers and visitors to read. Its wording should reflect the organization's activities and size of operation. The aim should be to produce a document that employees relate to and understand. This may mean that it has to be produced in Braille or a number of different languages depending on the backgrounds and skills of the staff. Ideally, employees should be asked to comment or contribute. The statement should declare the organization's commitment to meet all the relevant requirements (including legal and stakeholder needs) and to review and continually improve its performance. An example is shown in the text box overleaf.

The policy should be written in such a way that it enables meaningful objectives to be established and reviewed. A mission statement is not a bad starting point, but for that to be translated into something that is more than a wish list it needs a statement of policy. A company policy statement should not be specific to quality, environment or anything else; rather it should commit the company to those practices and principles that are relevant to it.

Such a general policy might read as follows.

Management policy

It is the policy of this organization to follow the best management practices with the object of achieving continual improvement to the benefit of all our stakeholders. We shall abide by all relevant legislation and other requirements to which we subscribe. In particular, we will meet the requirements of the management system standards, guides and other documents listed at the foot of this statement; these will be regularly reviewed together with this policy.

This statement of policy will be communicated to all employees and made available to all interested parties.

Planning (Clause 4.3)

4.3.1 Identification and evaluation of aspects, impacts and risks
4.3.2 Identification of legal and other requirements
4.3.3 Contingency planning
4.3.4 Objectives
4.3.5 Organizational structure, roles, responsibilities and authorities

This phase (particularly 4.3.1) is the core of the system. It is where the scope and the needs of the management system are determined. This gives rise to the objectives and targets to meet the needs of interested parties and the resources required.

Subclause 4.3.1 uses the word 'aspects' to cover in generic terms the critical issues that need to be controlled in any process to ensure a satisfactory outcome. For instance, it is essential that a 24-hour cash machine has money available as part of a banking cash provision service and that the money is paid out to customers using the service within a reasonable time.

One of the most convenient methods for integrating your assessment of the needs and scope of the IMS is to establish the processes involved in the operation of the organization. Then the aspects can be identified, as shown in Figure 9.1.

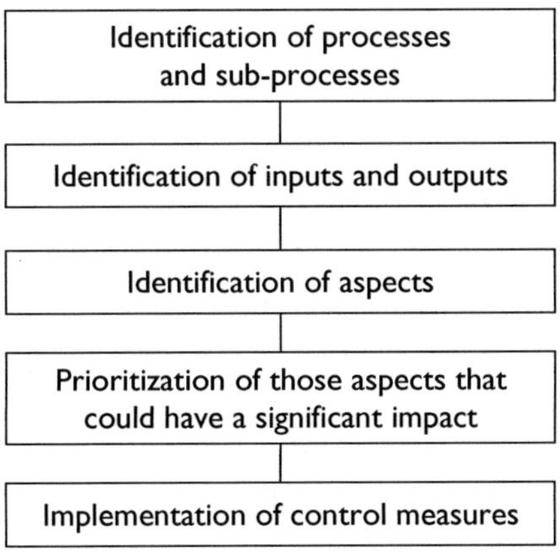

Figure 9.1 – Identifying the aspects

Anything an organization does can be considered a process. An advice centre has a process of gathering and disseminating information. A manufacturer will buy in raw materials and supply finished goods. These processes have, in practice, many sub-processes. In simple terms a process can be as shown in Figure 9.2.

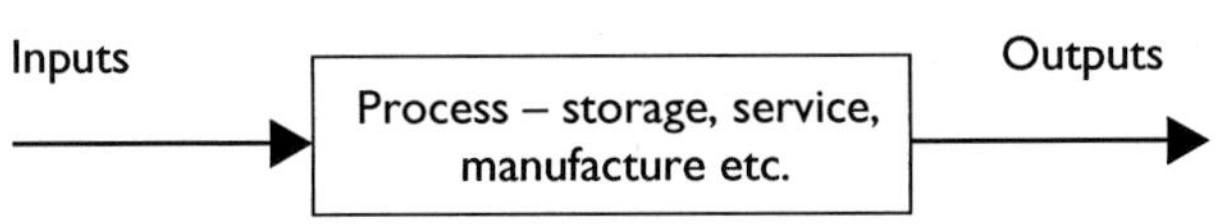

Figure 9.2 – A simple process

These processes may have many components with inputs and outputs, so an organization may be considered in the way shown in Figure 9.3.

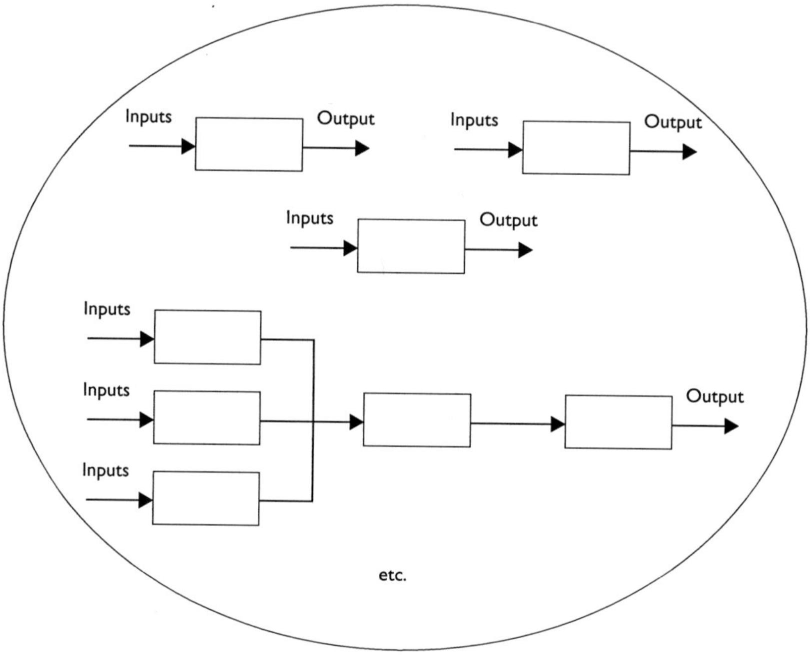

Figure 9.3 – A series of processes within an organization

This sort of approach should be used when considering all the activities under the control or influence of the organization, including purchasing, maintenance, storage, disposal, usage etc., as well as the main service/manufacturing activities.

The process then has to be evaluated to determine the aspects.

Identification and prioritization of significant aspects

We all recognize that the future is uncertain but we work on the assumption that tomorrow will be much the same as today and the conditions under which we work will not be significantly different. We recognize that there might be an earthquake or that an airliner might crash into our offices, but we rate such occurrences as very unlikely and in any case there is not much we could do to prepare for them. In practice there are many other less spectacular risks that we accept every day. There are strategic risks – will our customers continue to buy our products or will new technology/ fashion/social trends/political pressures erode the demand? These are matters for the highest level of management to consider. Then there are risks at the managerial level – do we rely on a new supplier that is much cheaper but in a country prone to unrest? And there are risks at the operational level – do we use the new supplies that we urgently need even though the inspection results are not through yet?

There are many risks involved in the day-to-day operation of an organization but they are not always perceived as 'risks'. Here we use the word 'aspect' to describe those facets of a process that could pose a threat. Risks are evaluated in order to prioritize the aspects, for action to be taken to control them.

Some of the existing management system standards give a process for identifying the aspects that are specific to that management system discipline. Some organizations will wish to continue using their established processes and there is nothing wrong in such an approach. This book recommends a generic approach that enables the aspects to be determined in a similar manner – no matter the management discipline.

Having established a flow diagram and all the processes involved, each process needs to be reviewed as to whether it has an aspect that might potentially lead to quality problems, significant environmental impacts or a health and safety risk. This process can be very time-consuming but is fundamental to the process. The size of the task may appear daunting, but it can be more manageable if you make a quick appraisal of each process to prioritize them for evaluation. If you have identified 100 processes it makes sense to concentrate on those 10 to 20 where there may be significant aspects. This does not mean the other processes should be discounted, unless it is obvious that the aspects are trivial.

This approach has many advantages. Not least is the fact that if used sensibly, involving employees at the operational end, the approach should help engender a positive culture and result in ownership of the control measures that need to be implemented.

Subclause 4.3.1 recognizes the need to prioritize the aspects. In the example given of the cash machine, money availability is obviously the priority and the timing issue has some flexibility.

Simultaneously with the identification process there is benefit in prioritizing – even if it is only a first estimate. This enables the trivial and the low-risk aspects to be ignored and the significant aspects to be targeted.

Here again there is advantage in using a common approach, as long as it does not conflict with well-established processes. The use of the simple matrix approach in Figure 9.4, as a first pass, helps to keep the effort proportionate to the risk and avoids excessive effort in one discipline. Risk is seen as having two dimensions. The risk of the aspect having a significant impact is dependent on the likelihood of the event happening and the consequence.

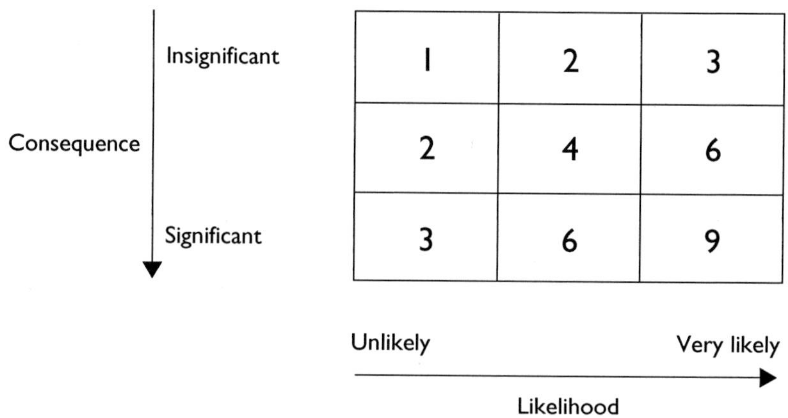

Figure 9.4 – A simple matrix to help in prioritization

Matrices such as this are commonly used for ranking in OH&S and sometimes in environmental management. Here it is recommended that the common axes are 'likelihood' and 'consequence'. The latter needs to be considered in a number of ways depending on the discipline: significant quality aspects may mean product recall, for instance, whilst significant environmental aspects may mean a major toxic spillage or loss of resource.

Using the matrix in Figure 9.4 it is possible to identify as a group those processes or stages of a process that could cause a major quality defect, lead to major ill health or a serious accident, a major environmental incident, or shortage of material. The process used to identify the aspects and prioritization should be recorded/documented in some manner and those aspects that are considered significant should be listed.

Action to deal with the significant aspects needs to be considered in the light of:

- the number of significant aspects;
- the likelihood of immediate serious repercussions in the absence of action;
- financial loss;
- regulatory requirements.

It is obvious that some will need to be addressed urgently while others can be dealt with over a period of time. If, for instance, emission controls mean that new plant has to be installed then an investment plan will need to be developed and the total time involved may be many months or years. If commitment is to be gained for the new IMS, it is preferable to identify at least one aspect to be tackled that involves employees being actively engaged at an early stage.

Other planning issues

The identification of legal and other requirements (4.3.2) and contingency planning (4.3.3) follow aspect, impact and risk identification. This assists in the selection of objectives (4.3.4) and developing the plan is the next stage. Obviously there is a need to identify resources. In the first place commitment at the highest level to the IMS is imperative and essential to the achievement of the key objectives. This establishment of authority and accountability needs to be understood and agreed throughout the chain of command responsible for delivering the objectives.

Subclause 4.3.5 then seeks to establish the plan for implementing the operational measures for controlling and achieving the policy, objectives and targets that have been established using the resources and authorities defined.

Contingency planning (4.3.3) is not an element that is readily identified in all management system standards. What it seeks to establish is that the organization formalizes its arrangements for dealing with such aspects as a major recall of products, fires, floods etc. It also seeks to establish arrangements to mitigate foreseeable emergencies and continuity arrangements should the unthinkable happen. The need for such an arrangement is obviously appreciated by some organizations with ISO 9001 but it is not strongly identified within the standard as a key element. Some other standards recognize this as 'emergency preparedness and response'.

Implementation and operation (Clause 4.4)

4.4.1 Operational control
4.4.2 Management of resources
4.4.3 Documentation requirements
4.4.4 Communication

This is the 'do' part of the process. It is the actual implementation and operation of the key processes and control measures that are seen as essential to the organization's success. Operational control (4.4.1) requires that the organization ensures that the objectives and requirements are being met and, moreover, that the necessary support processes, resources and documentation are provided and verified, validated, monitored etc. as appropriate.

In the past many systems have been paper-based with little real management commitment and with targets set that were unrealistic given the resources allocated. Subclause 4.4.2 recognizes this and seeks to ensure that the requirements of 4.3.1 (identify and evaluate aspects) are delivered. Subclause 4.4.2 asks that the skills base is provided, that there are processes for validating that this is the case, and that personnel understand what is expected of them individually and collectively.

Subclause 4.4.2 seeks to ensure that what applies to people also applies to the other resources needed to implement effective operational control. This includes buildings, maintenance, materials, communication, transport etc.

Many management systems have traditionally been document-driven and slavish adherence to this facet has sometimes been seen as fundamental to, rather than supportive of the management system. The aim should be to provide the infrastructure and framework for documentation, document control and records that are essential for the effective and efficient operation of the system. Anything more will fail to meet these requirements. It is now common to use flow diagrams and computer-based systems, which can help mitigate those activities that have traditionally been time-consuming and exacting. Nevertheless, these areas are very important, and subclauses 4.4.3 and 4.4.4 identify what is needed. Remember the golden rule for the IMS to work and not to be a tome of unused paperwork:

Keep it simple. Document and record only what is necessary. Do not let the documents drive the system.

Communication (4.4.4) is a key element. The degree of communication needed will depend on the scope of the system. In the case of information security, there may well be a need for very restricted communication on some subjects. For environmental management there may well be a need for a wide and transparent communication system. The IMS needs to contain this element but it may need considerable tailoring for the different disciplines within the overall system.

All organizations will have some need to interface with suppliers, whether internal or external. Subclause 4.4.4 recognizes that this control applies to all management system areas equally, not just to quality where it has a dominant role.

Performance assessment (Clause 4.5)

4.5.1 Monitoring and measurement
4.5.2 Evaluation of compliance
4.5.3 Internal audit
4.5.4 Handling of nonconformities

This element does not appear as such in existing standards on management systems. However, it is becoming increasingly recognized that management systems that just generate a certificate on the wall are costly to maintain and give very little benefit. If a management system is to be recognized as being of value to the organization and to the stakeholder, then the outputs must demonstrate its effectiveness. It is widely accepted that if you cannot measure it you cannot manage it. Subclauses 4.5.1, 4.5.2 and 4.5.3 establish the need to monitor and measure, analyse failures and audit the system. These activities are seen as being interlinked but discrete actions in their own right. In the case of subclauses 4.5.1 and 4.5.3 they need to be established as regular programmes. These processes are well understood by those familiar with management systems and more information on how to undertake these activities is given in publications such as ISO 9004, ISO 14004, BS 8800 and ISO 14031.

Improvement (Clause 4.6)

4.6.1 General
4.6.2 Corrective, preventive and improvement action

There is now a key requirement specified in ISO 9001, which has always been understood, that the aim should be to continually improve.

The need for corrective action arises when there has been some failure in the system; preventive action should be needed only rarely when there has been a failure in identifying aspects and risks.

Subclause 4.6.2 emphasizes the need to encompass all the issues that arise with regard to improving the overall management system.

Management review (Clause 4.7)

4.7.1 General
4.7.2 Input
4.7.3 Output

At first sight the value of the review may be questioned given that continual improvement has already been mentioned. There is an important difference: continual improvement (4.6.2) is the process for improving the current management system, while management review goes very much further. It is a process that needs to be carried out periodically to establish whether what you have in place can deliver your needs. The current system may be working perfectly but maybe cannot cope with emerging circumstances – for example if the organization has diversified its business.

10. Getting started

Initial status review

The way forward for those seeking to implement an IMS is to establish what existing arrangements are in place and the gap between those and the sub-element requirements shown in Appendix 1. This simple gap analysis approach will ensure effort is not wasted on developing new systems when existing arrangements are working well. There will of course need to be an identification of the significant aspects where controls are needed, as described in the previous chapter and in 4.3.5 of PAS 99.

Even those organizations that may believe they have nothing in place will find that certain jobs follow some long-established 'standard operating procedures', or that emergency procedures exist. Such arrangements may need reviewing in the fullness of time but in the first stage they can be given a lower priority than those processes where the significant aspects have not been identified and/or controlled effectively.

A simple way forward is to follow the approach shown earlier in Figures 9.1 and 9.3. The identification of key processes and the significant aspects, relating to the discipline covered within the IMS, enables a review to be carried out of the existing arrangements for control measures. For each of the significant aspects a matrix of the existing arrangements and shortfalls gives a visual gap analysis, as shown in Table 10.1.

Table 10.1 – A gap analysis chart

Element	Sub-element	Significant aspect			
		1	2	3	etc.
0	Management system				
1 Policy	Policy and principles				
2 Planning	Identification of business risks				
3 etc.					

11. Integrating management systems into your IMS

Integrating a quality system into your IMS

The core PAS 99 outline (see Appendix 1) contains many similar clauses to those found in the ISO 9001 standard with the word 'quality' omitted, so the amendments/additions to the framework needed to accommodate quality management are minimal. Most of the 'common' elements are included in the framework and the process of deciding which aspects have a significant impact will need to be addressed in these common elements or separately. For instance, if it is decided that design is a process that needs to be controlled, the ISO 9001 element on this facet should be embraced within the IMS.

For a step-by-step guide on how to implement and/or integrate a quality system within an IMS framework, other books in this series will help you.

For reference purposes the matrix given in Appendix 2 demonstrates where the ISO 9001 elements fit in the IMS framework and which need to be treated as specific elements outside the common elements.

Integrating an environmental system into your IMS

Environmental management system ISO 14001 is based on a PDCA process very much like the model used here. There is a slight difference in order. As with quality, much of the environmental management arrangements can be embraced within the common elements of the framework. ISO 14001 refers to procedures rather than processes but lends itself very much to the process approach within the PDCA framework.

The uniqueness is the identification of environmental aspects and the legal requirements. As can be seen in the second publication in this series (*IMS: Implementing and Operating Using PAS 99*) the risk-based approach allows a common approach for identification of aspects whether they are environmental, quality or OH&S (risks).

Although the language used in the framework is mainly based on that used in ISO 9001, those familiar with ISO 14001 will find many commonalities. There are additions needed; the matrix in Appendix 2 highlights the major shortfalls.

Environmental regulatory requirements are at several levels, including international conventions, national and regional regulations and local by-laws.

Integrating an OH&S system into your IMS

As with environmental management, the structure of BS OHSAS 18001 is based on PDCA and has a structure similar to that of ISO 14001. Nearly all the points made in relation to integrating an environmental system apply to OH&S management systems.

However, there is a legal requirement in many countries to carry out a risk assessment and to implement controls, therefore the legal compliance issue needs to be addressed in the light of the local regulations.

Integrating an information security system into your IMS

The structure of this standard (BS ISO/IEC 27001, BS 7799-2) is very different to the others but it also is risk-based and lends itself to the same approach.

The major issue, as in all of the other systems, is the identification of aspects. In this field it is particularly challenging, with the number of hackers trying to breach IT systems, for instance. There are many unknowns to evaluate. The matrix in Appendix 2 gives you some idea of where the common elements match.

Details of how to implement such a system can be found in *IMS: Information Security*.

Integrating other systems

There are many other areas that need to be managed, such as food hygiene in the food industry (HACCP), risk management, corporate governance and customer satisfaction. All these processes can be handled in a similar way and other books in this series address these issues. (See *Managing Food Safety the 22000 Way* – which uses the PAS 99 model for integration.)

Appendix 1. The PAS 99 framework

Clause 4: The main elements and sub-elements

4.1 General requirements
4.2 Management system policy
4.3 Planning
- *4.3.1 Identification and evaluation of aspects, impacts and risks*
- *4.3.2 Identification of legal and other requirements*
- *4.3.3 Contingency planning*
- *4.3.4 Objectives*
- *4.3.5 Organizational structure, roles, responsibilities and authorities*

4.4 Implementation and operation
- *4.4.1 Operational control*
- *4.4.2 Management of resources*
- *4.4.3 Documentation requirements*
- *4.4.4 Communication*

4.5 Performance assessment
- *4.5.1 Monitoring and measurement*
- *4.5.2 Evaluation of compliance*
- *4.5.3 Internal audit*
- *4.5.4 Handling of nonconformities*

4.6 Improvement
- *4.6.1 General*
- *4.6.2 Corrective, preventive and improvement action*

4.7 Management review
- *4.7.1 General*
- *4.7.2 Input*
- *4.7.3 Output*

(For full definitions refer to PAS 99.)

Appendix 2. Common requirements

Common requirements of quality, environmental management and health and safety management

Requirements of PAS 99	ISO 9001 Quality clause	ISO 14001 Environmental management clause	OHSAS 18001* Health and safety clause
4.1 General requirements	4.1	4.1	4.1
4.2 Management system policy	5.1, 5.3	4.2	4.2
4.3 Planning		4.3	4.3
4.3.1 Identification and evaluation of aspects, impacts and risks	5.2, 5.4.2, 7.2.1, 7.2.2	4.3.1	4.3.1
4.3.2 Identification of legal and other requirements	5.3(b). 7.2.1(c)	4.3.2	4.3.2
4.3.3 Contingency planning	8.3	4.4.7	4.4.7
4.3.4 Objectives	5.4.1	4.3.3	4.3.3
4.3.5 Organizational structure, roles, responsibilities and authorities	5.5	4.4.1	4.4.1
4.4 Implementation and operation			
4.4.1 Operational control	7	4.4.6	4.4.6
4.4.2 Management of resources	6	4.4.1, 4.4.2	4.4.1, 4.4.2
4.4.3 Documentation requirements	4.2	4.4.4, 4.4.5, 4.5.4	4.4.4, 4.4.5, 4.5.3

4.4.4 Communication	5.5.3, 7.2.3, 5.3(d), 5.5.1	4.4.3	4.4.3
4.5 Performance assessment			
4.5.1 Monitoring and measurement	8.1	4.5.1	4.5.1
4.5.2 Evaluation of compliance	8.2.4	4.5.2	4.5.1
4.5.3 Internal audit	8.2.2	4.5.5	4.5.4
4.5.4 Handling of nonconformities	8.3	4.5.3	4.5.2
4.6 Improvement			
4.6.1 General	8.5.1	4.5.3	4.5.2
4.6.2 Corrective, preventive and improvement action	8.5.2, 8.5.3	4.5.3	4.5.2
4.7 Management Review			
4.7.1 General	5.6.1	4.6	4.6
4.7.2 Input	5.6.2		
4.7.3 Output	5.6.3		
* Since the publication of PAS 99 a new version of OHSAS 18001 has been published: BS OHSAS 18001:2007			

Adapted from: PAS 99, p.18

Common requirements of information technology, security systems and food safety

Requirements of PAS 99	ISO/IEC 20000 IT Service management specification clause	ISO/IEC 27001 Information security clause	ISO 22000 Food safety clause
4.1 General requirements	3	4.1, 4.2	4.1
4.2 Management system policy	3.1, 4.4.1	5.1	5.1, 5.2
4.3 Planning	4.1	4.2	5.3
4.3.1 Identification and evaluation of aspects, impacts and risks	4.1(f), 4.2(d)	4.2	5.3, 7.1, 7.2, 7.3, 7.4

4.3.2 Identification of legal and other requirements		4.2.1 (b2)	7.2.3
4.3.3 Contingency planning	8.2		3.3, 5.7, 7.10, 7.10.4
4.3.4 Objectives	4.1(b), 5.0	4.2.2	7.5, 7.6
4.3.5 Organizational structure, roles, responsibilities and authorities	4.2	4.2.2	5
4.4 Implementation and operation			
4.4.1 Operational control	4.2, 6.0	4.2.2	7.7, 7.8, 7.9
4.4.2 Management of resources	3.1, 3.3	5.2.1, 5.2.2	5.1, 5.3, 5.4, 5.5, 6.1, 6.2
4.4.3 Documentation requirements	3.2	4.3	4.2
4.4.4 Communication	3.1(b), 7	4.2.4(c)	5.6
4.5 Performance assessment			
4.5.1 Monitoring and measurement	4.3	4.2.3	7.6.4, 7.6.5, 8.3
4.5.2 Evaluation of compliance	4.3	4.2.3	8.4.3
4.5.3 Internal audit	4.3	6	8.4.1
4.5.4 Handling of nonconformities	4.3	4.2.4	7.6.5, 7.10
4.6 Improvement			
4.6.1 General	4.4	4.2.4, 8.1	8.1, 8.5
4.6.2 Corrective, preventive and improvement action	4.2.4(b), 8.2, 8.3	8.2, 8.3	8.2
4.7 Management Review			
4.7.1 General	3.1(g)	7.1	5.8, 8.5.2
4.7.2 Input		7.2	5.8.2
4.7.3 Output		7.3	5.8.3

Source: PAS 99, p.19

Bibliography

Standards and specifications

BS 8800:2004, *Occupational health and safety management systems — Guide*

BS 8900:2006, *Guidance for managing sustainable development*

BS EN ISO 22000:2005, *Food safety management systems — Requirements for any organization in the food chain*

BS ISO/IEC 27001:2005, BS 7799-2:2005, *Information technology — Security techniques — Code of practice for information security management*

BS ISO/IEC 20000:2005, *Information technology — Service management — Part 1: Specification*

BS ISO/IEC 27001:2005, BS 7799-2:2005, *Information technology — Security techniques — Information security management systems — Requirements*

BS OHSAS 18001:2007, *Occupational health and safety management systems — Requirements*

ISO 9000:2005, *Quality management systems — Fundamentals and vocabulary*

ISO 9001:2000, *Quality management systems — Requirements*

ISO 9004:2000, *Quality management systems — Guidelines for performance improvements*

ISO 14001:2004, *Environmental management systems — Requirements with guidance for use*

ISO 14004:2004, *Environmental management systems — General guidelines on principles, systems and support techniques*

ISO 14031:2000, *Environmental management — Environmental performance evaluation — Guidelines*

ISO/CD 31000: to be published, *General guidelines for principles and implementation of risk management*

ISO/IEC Guide 73:2002, *Risk management — Vocabulary — Guidelines for use in standards*

PAS 99:2006, *Specification of common management system requirements as a framework for integration*

Other publications

Hinch, H (2003) *IMS: Managing Food Safety,* BSI, London
IMS Risk Solutions (2003) *IMS: Creating a Manual,* BSI, London
Karapetrovic et al. (2006) *Dynamics and integration of standardized management systems,* Documentaria Universitaria, Universitat de Girona
MacGregor Associates (1997) *Management System Standards* (HB 10138), BSI, London
Murray, P (2003) *IMS: Information Security,* BSI, London
Smith, D (2001) *IMS: The Framework,* BSI, London
Smith, D and Politowski, R (2007) *IMS: Implementing and Operating Using PAS 99,* BSI, London
Integrated Management Systems (IMS) – Potential Safety Benefits Achievable from Integrated Management of Safety, Health, Environment and Quality (SHE&Q), (2005) Organisation for Economic Co-operation and Development, Paris
Smith, D Politowski, R Palmer, C (2007). *Managing Food Safety the ISO 22000 Way,* BSI, London